Vegetarian Quick & Easy
Under 15 Minutes

Vegetarian Quick & Easy Under 15 Minutes

100 Simple Natural Foods Recipes

By

Jonathan Vine

From the author

Whether you are a novice or an expert in the kitchen, you won't need more than 15 minutes to make these recipes! Impressing your family and loved ones has never been easier!

Time may be precious, but so is food. We need it not only to survive but also to bring us joy and great taste experiences, to challenge our taste buds with new flavors, and, last but not least, to nourish us. But what do you do when you only have 15 minutes at your disposal? Time management is the answer. And that is what this book offers you—recipes that don't take more than 15 minutes to make, without sacrificing any of the taste.

What's your part in all this? Just put on that apron and go to the kitchen. Have fun and enjoy cooking! Believe me, food that took hours to prepare but was done without any kind of passion won't taste better than food prepared in just 15 minutes with all the love in your heart.

Vegetarian Quick & Easy- Under 15 Minutes \ Jonathan Vine

Editor: Hofit Carmi

ISBN: 978-965-92331-3-7

Copyright© 2014 by Jonathan Vine
All rights reserved. No part of this book may be reproduced or transmitted in any form or by any means, electronic, or mechanical, including photocopying, recording or by any information storage and retrieval system without permission in writing.

Contact Information: jonathanvinebooks@gmail.com

Publisher: www.ebook-pro.com

DISCLAIMER
The information presented in this book represents the views of the publisher as of the date of publication. The publisher reserves the rights to alter and update their opinions based on new conditions. This book is for informational purposes only. The author and publisher do not accept any responsibilities for any liabilities resulting from the use of this information. While every attempt has been made to verify the information provided here, the author and the publisher cannot assume any responsibility for errors, inaccuracies or omissions.

CONTENTS

INTRODUCTION — 10

What is a Vegetarian? — 10
The Benefits of Being Vegetarian — 12
Becoming a Vegetarian — 15
Time Management and Being a Vegetarian — 16

EASY AND QUICK RECIPES FOR BUSY MUMS — 18

Spiced Breakfast Pudding — 19
Avocado Scramble — 20
Yogurt and Oatmeal Parfait — 21
Vanilla French Toast — 22
Cheesy Quesadillas — 24
Cheesy Dill Omelet — 25
Egg-In-Pepper — 26
Tomato and Avocado Sandwich — 27
Flat Bread Skillet Pizza — 28
Poached Tofu with Tomato Sauce — 30
Cilantro Tofu Fillets — 31
Quick Lettuce Wraps — 32
Cheesy Grits — 33
Cheesy Mushrooms — 34
Ricotta Cheese Fritters — 36
Fried Rice with Tomato — 37
Creamy Corn Soup — 38
Quick Burritos — 40
Italian Grilled Sandwich — 41
Guacamole Bites — 42
Summer Pasta Salad — 43
Caramel Apples — 44
Tempeh Reuben Sandwich — 46
Crunchy Zucchini Sauté — 47
Greek Salad — 48
Spinach and Broccoli Salad — 50
Rice and Egg Salad — 51
Tortillas Filled with Cream Cheese — 52
Sweet Potato Thyme Hash — 53
Potato Pancakes — 54

QUICK AND EASY RECIPES FOR ROMANTIC MEALS — 57

Granola Parfait — 58
Nutella French Toast — 59
Pesto Omelet — 60
Nutella Trifle — 61
Caprese Salad — 62
Grilled Tofu Steak with Kale Sauté — 65
Spinach and Strawberry Balsamic Salad — 68
Roasted Bell Pepper Soup — 69
Chili Pecorino Spaghetti — 70
Spiced Sautéed Mushrooms — 71
Sage Gnocchi — 72
Lentil and Cucumber Salad — 74
Spinach and Ricotta Raw Lasagna — 75
Shakshouka – Tomato Poached Eggs — 76
Three-Cheese Pasta — 78
Cheese-Filled Croissants — 79
Battered Tofu — 80
Tofu Piccata — 81
Chocolate Fondue — 82
Lemon Flavored Roasted Asparagus — 84
Sweet and Spicy Tofu Stir Fry — 85
Tofu and Ginger Soup — 86
Tofu au Vin — 87
Poached Brussels Sprouts with Parmesan Topping — 88
Caramel Pears — 90
Cheesecake Bites — 91
Minty Fruit Salad Cups — 92
Grilled Peaches with Raspberry Sorbet — 94

QUICK AND EASY RECIPES THAT EVEN KIDS CAN MAKE — 95

Pita Pockets	96
Egg Cups	97
Colorful Quinoa	98
Nutella Popsicles	99
Gazpacho – Cold Tomato Soup	100
Date and Coconut Bites	102
Carrots and Herbed Cream Cheese Dip	103
Warm Peanut Butter and Banana Sandwich	104
Cheesy Black Bean Tacos	106
Pizza Sandwiches	107
Peanut Butter Dip with Apple and Pears	108
Hot Chocolate Mix	109
Dark Chocolate Clusters	110
Homemade Cereals	112
Marshmallow Pops	113
Chocolate Chip Parfait	114
Chocolate Chip and Raspberry Snacks	115
Italian Flavored Popcorn	116
Beet and Berry Smoothie	117
Strawberry and Spinach Smoothie	118

EASY AND QUICK RECIPES FOR PARTIES — 120

Tortilla Wheels	121
Quick Banana Popsicles	122
Marshmallow Sauce and Fruit Skewers	123
Mini Pita Pizzas	124
Sticky Rice Balls	125
Red Wine Punch	126
Mexican Vegetarian Sushi	128
Deviled Eggs	129
Spicy Cheese Fondue	130
Two-Layer Hummus	131
Olive Oil and Fresh Ricotta Bruschetta	133
Spicy White Bean Dip with Tortilla Chips	134
Basil, Watermelon and Feta Bites	135
Parmesan and Basil Tomato Bites	136
Endive Boats	137
Scallion Goat Cheese Balls	138
Potato Chip Snacks	139
Spicy Pecans	140
Blue Cheese and Pear Crostini	141
Walnut and Cheese-Stuffed Figs	142

CONCLUSION — 144

Introduction

Leading a vegetarian lifestyle is becoming more and more popular nowadays, and I assume that if you are reading this book, you belong to that category. Or, at least, you're interested in finding out what it's all about. However, not many people do it the right way or for the right reasons. So let's have a look at what being vegetarian means, how you can go vegetarian, what foods you can eat, and how it affects your life and health.

What is a Vegetarian?

Generally, a vegetarian is a person who doesn't eat beef, fish, poultry, or any other animal products such as lard, chicken stock, or gelatin. A vegetarian's diet mainly consists of vegetables, fruits, legumes, grains, seeds, nuts, and sometimes eggs and dairy products as well. But this description is very general. If we were to go into detail, I would say that vegetarians can be classified into three groups:

- Total vegetarians are also known as vegans; they don't eat beef, fish, poultry, eggs, or dairy, not even honey, and definitely no chicken stock or gelatin. Sometimes, vegans go raw as well, meaning that they only eat food in its natural form—raw—believing that it's the only way to preserve all the nutrients.
- Lactovegetarians exclude all meats and eggs but include dairy products.
- Lacto-ovo-vegetarians do not eat meat, fish, or poultry but allow eggs and dairy.

In the end, a vegetarian is a person who is willing to give up eating meat to find healthier alternatives for proteins.

People become vegetarians for many reasons, but the most common ones are:
- Health – certain diseases, such as diabetes, eating disorders, weight problems, or heart problems, can be stopped or reversed through a healthy diet and lifestyle.
- Environment – animals are very important for an ecosystem, especially if we're talking about wild animals that are hunted and killed for their meat. Some of them have been hunted so much that they are now close to extinction, and that is very sad and unfortunate for the environment.
- Economic – meat can be rather expensive, especially if it's good quality. Giving up on meat is just one way to reduce the budget, but it is worth considering because it is also beneficial for your health.
- Compassion – people who love animals as much as they love people feel compassion for the animals killed for food. However, I'm not suggesting that people who eat meat don't love animals. It is a matter of personal belief, and every individual should address the issue according to his or her conscience.
- Spiritual or religious reasons – the diet that accompanies certain religious holidays in certain countries around the globe is a vegetarian diet, and many people adopt that diet out of religious or spiritual beliefs.

The Benefits of Being Vegetarian

According to many studies and experts, vegetarians have a low risk of developing heart disease, cancer, diabetes, obesity, high blood pressure, skin problems, acne, or eating disorders.

But why does that happen, and what does it mean? First of all, a vegetarian diet is based on fresh fruits and vegetables, which have a high nutritional content from vitamins to antioxidants and fibers.

One of the main concerns about going vegetarian is whether you will get enough nutrients, but let's be realistic and think for a second. Vegetables and fruits have everything from proteins to antioxidants, fiber, and minerals while meat has mainly proteins. Now, you choose which option is the best! I sure find fruits and veggies to be a healthier choice; in addition, they are much more versatile and easier to cook. In fact, after going vegetarian, many people discover that they have many more options than they had when they ate meat as well.

The key is to eat a wide variety of foods and try to include all sorts of nutrients:
- Proteins – protein is the main component of our skin, hair, and nails, and we need it to be healthy, but meat is not the only source of proteins. Spinach, kale, soy, beans, sun-dried tomatoes, sprouts, broccoli, and peas are some of the most common and delicious options. It's such a long and varied list!
- Calcium – it is recommended to consume at least 1000mg of calcium per day—the equivalent of three cups of milk or yogurt. Now, milk and yogurt are allowed in a vegetarian diet, but there are other great calcium sources, such as

green leafy vegetables, broccoli, beans, figs, sunflower seeds, and cereals. Vegetarians must include at least two portions of these into their daily diet to meet the needed calcium requirements every day.
- Vitamin D – vitamin D is what helps calcium absorb and set into bones or teeth. Your body can make its own vitamin D, but eating foods that have a high content of it helps greatly, especially during the winter months. Soy, dairy products, and eggs are just a few good sources of vitamin D.
- Iron – iron helps with the production of hemoglobin and blood cells, and that makes it crucial for preventing anemia. It can be found in cereals, dried fruits, molasses, sesame seeds, soybeans, and dark leafy vegetables. But don't forget that you also need a high amount of vitamin C to help your body absorb the iron.
- Vitamin B-12 – this vitamin is found in animal products, but also in dairy and eggs. People who choose to eat dairy and eggs with their vegetarian diet get plenty of vitamin B-12. Vegans, however, may have a hard time getting enough of it and sometimes need vitamin B-12 supplements.

The benefits of a vegetarian life include:
- A healthier body and mind – as I stated above, a vegetarian diet is rich in vitamins and nutrients, and that is enough to detox your body and improve your long-term health.
- Weight control– once you go vegetarian, you obviously reduce the amount of fat and sugar you eat and focus more on fresh products. This leads to weight loss, but in order to keep it that way, you need to continue eating vegetarian and keep your diet as balanced as possible by including a variety of foods into your daily menu.

- A longer life span – switching from a fatty, sugary diet to a vegetarian one is definitely an improvement that will boost your health, cleanse your system of toxins, and increase your life span by at least a few years. It has been proven that people who focus more on fruits and veggies and less on meat live longer lives.
- Strong bones – worry not; fruits and veggies have plenty of calcium, and you will have full access to them. In fact, they contain more calcium than any dairy product on the market!
- Relief from allergies and intolerances – allergies are unforgiving and affect many people around the globe, from kids to grown-ups. The solution to relieve these allergic reactions is a healthy diet based on plenty of nutrients to strengthen your immune system and flush out the toxins.
- More energy – good nutrition generates more energy—energy to play with the kids, to go for walks, to go out and dance, to have fun, to go to work, and everything else you've ever wanted to do.
- Fiber – fiber is crucial for your digestive system, but a vegetarian diet solves that problem. Once you begin to add more fiber into your diet, you will notice less bloating and faster digestion.
- Sparing animals – over 10 billion animals are killed each year for human consumption. They go through a scary process and are killed without mercy in order to feed people across the globe.
- Colorful meals – once you take that meat off the plate, you will be left with a wide range of veggies, colorful and fun, all having different tastes and textures. That is a real eating experience, in my opinion.

Becoming a Vegetarian

No diet change is easy, especially when you have already tasted meat, but it's not impossible. So many people have done it already. You can do it too, and here are a few tips to guide you through:

- Identify your reasons and make sure they're true and strong. You will no doubt face temptations, and that is the point where you have to remind yourself of the reasons you chose to go vegetarian. Make it clear for yourself that this is what you want and nothing else will do.
- Read and inform yourself as much as possible. Information is power, people say, and it couldn't be truer!
- Seek help if you feel overwhelmed. Friends and family all need to know you are doing this, so ask for their support. You can also talk to a nutritionist about your concerns and get proper advice.
- Find and try new recipes. Boredom rarely happens with a vegetarian diet because there are so many ways to cook a simple vegetable like a potato. Always look for new recipes and new combinations; always be open to new aromas and always try new recipes, without forgetting the old ones. A cookbook is a great place to start, but remember that no recipe is set in stone. Be creative and go exploring on your own too.
- Customize your old recipes. Choose an old recipe you enjoyed before and find substitutions. Tofu is a great option to replace meat, but there are many other ways to do the same thing. Just look for them!
- Dairy and eggs can make the transition from a meat diet to a vegetarian diet much easier. They are easy to cook and can easily be customized, so consider this kind of diet before going extreme vegetarian.
- Give up meat all at once go or gradually. It's up to you how you do it. Just go for it and never forget your reasons. Have fun and enjoy the whole process. This way, you will get the results you are hoping for.

Time Management and Being a Vegetarian

Time is precious these days. I look around and notice so many people hurrying to work, hurrying to school, in a rush to see their families, and so on. They don't have much time for themselves, let alone for cooking. But that doesn't mean you have to eat whatever! Definitely not! It means that you just have to plan your time better and use a book like this to save your life.

Here are some shortcuts that will help you get organized and actually find time to cook for yourself and your family:
- Make a shopping list – before going shopping, check your fridge and pantry and buy things you can stock up on such as crackers, flour, and sugar; and purchase vegetables or fruits that can be stored for longer periods of time like potatoes, apples, oranges, and fennel. Frozen vegetables are a good option, and some of them, like corn and green peas, actually taste better once frozen. They are a lifesaver, believe me!
- Buy canned foods – beans, chickpeas, and lentils are great canned and save you the time it would take to cook them at home, so don't be afraid to buy them already cooked in a can.
- Plana menu for the whole week – weekends are surely more relaxed, so take a few minutes to talk to your family and decide what they want to eat for the next week. A plan like this will help you shop for the ingredients you need and will save you even more time.

- Buy plenty of dried fruits and seeds to eat as snacks. Temptation is strong, and that is where these fruits and seeds come in. Chew them when you feel the need for junk food or meat, and the craving will go away.
- Stock up on pasta of all sorts. Pasta can be stored for months and comes in a wide variety of shapes and tastes. Always have pasta in your pantry!
- Whole grain cereals – they are a life saver for breakfast. Just check the label before buying and make sure they are organic and free of any toxins or additives.

Easy and Quick Recipes for Busy Mums

Being a mum is not an easy job, but it is so rewarding. Children are the biggest fulfillment of any woman, but they also take up most of her time. They have needs that keep mums busy all day long, especially when they are young. That is when time seems to be shorter and shorter, and mums are often put in a position where they have no choice but to give in and order some take out.

But those days are over because now you have, in your hands, a book full of amazing, delicious, and flavorful recipes to cook for your family without the hassle of long cooking times. I'm sure you can find 15 spare minutes between nursing your child and bathing him to cook a delicious lunch or dinner. I'm sure the rest of the family will appreciate a warm, homemade meal once in a while. You can even get them to help—that is how easy these recipes are!

Spiced Breakfast Pudding

Kids love puddings, don't they?! But this recipe is not your usual, simple pudding. It combines healthy oats and plenty of spices without becoming overwhelming.

Serves: 2-4

Ingredients:

- ½ cup quick cooking barley
- ½ cup bulgur
- ¼ cup rolled oats
- 2 cups almond milk
- 2 tablespoons raisins
- 1 pinch nutmeg
- 3 tablespoons honey
- 1 pinch cinnamon powder

Directions:

1

Combine the barley with the bulgur, oats, raisins, and almond milk.

2

Add the honey, nutmeg, and cinnamon and cook the pudding for 20 minutes over low heat.

3

When done, remove from heat and spoon it into serving bowls.

4

If you want, you can top it with fresh fruit to serve.

Avocado Scramble

Egg scramble is a classic, but children love this dish because it's creamy and rich. And you should be happy because it's also very easy to make as well as versatile.

Serves: 2-4

Ingredients:

- 1 ripe avocado, peeled and cubed
- 2 tablespoons olive oil
- 5 eggs, beaten
- 1 tablespoon chopped chives
- Salt, pepper to taste

Directions:

1

Mix the eggs with salt and pepper to taste, as well as the chopped chives.

2

Heat the olive oil in a skillet and add the avocado. Sauté for 2-3 minutes, then pour in the eggs.

3

Cook on low heat, mixing all the time, until the eggs are set but still creamy.

4

Serve the scramble right away

Yogurt and Oatmeal Parfait

Parfaits are easy to make, and your kids will love them because they are healthy and colorful and can be made with their favorite fruits as well.

Serves: 2-4

Ingredients:
- 2 cups Greek style yogurt
- 2 tablespoons honey
- ¼ cup shredded coconut
- 1 cup rolled oats
- 1 cup fresh fruit of your choice, cut in smaller pieces

Directions:

1

Mix the yogurt and honey.

2

Mix the oats with the shredded coconut.

3

Take 2-4 serving glasses or bowls and layer the yogurt with the rolled oats and fresh fruits.

4

Serve right away or refrigerate for a few hours, even overnight.

Vanilla French Toast

French toast and a glass of milk is something I grew up with, but my favorite toast was, by far, the vanilla one because it was the most delicate. Plus, it can be combined with any jam or syrup, and that is something not to be neglected.

Serves: 4

Ingredients:

- 4 slices white bread
- 2 eggs
- ½ cup almond milk
- 1 teaspoon vanilla extract
- 4 tablespoons vegetable oil

Directions:

1

Beat the eggs with the milk and vanilla.

2

Heat the oil in a large frying pan.

3

When the oil is hot, dip each slice of bread into the egg mixture, and then carefully place it into the hot oil.

4

Fry the bread a few minutes on each side until golden brown.

5

Place the toast on paper towels and serve right away, while still warm.

Cheesy Quesadillas

Mexican food seems to be a common choice for parties because it is spicy and rich. The quesadilla is one of those dishes, and it is delicious and perfect as finger food at a party.

Serves: 4

Ingredients:

- 8 flour tortillas
- 2 cups grated cheddar cheese
- 1 cup grated Monterey Jack cheese
- ½ teaspoon chili flakes

Directions:

1. Top each of the 4 tortillas with a mix of grated cheese.
2. Sprinkle with chili flakes, then place the remaining 4 tortillas on top.
3. Heat a grill pan over medium heat and place the tortillas on the grill, cooking them on both sides until golden brown.
4. When done, remove from pan and cut in small triangles.
5. Place them on a platter and serve warm.

Cheesy Dill Omelet

Dill, cheese, and eggs taste great. You have to try this recipe to see for yourself. It's delicate, rich, and absolutely delicious, perfect for a great start to the day.

Serves: 2-4

Ingredients:
- 6 eggs
- 2 tablespoons heavy cream
- 2 tablespoons chopped dill
- Salt, pepper to taste
- 1 pinch nutmeg
- 2 tablespoons vegetable oil
- ½ cup grated cheddar

Directions:

1

Heat the oil in a large frying pan or skillet.

2

In the meantime, beat the eggs until frothy, then add the heavy cream and dill. Season with salt and pepper and add a pinch of nutmeg.

3

Pour the egg mixture into the hot oil and fry until golden brown on one side, then flip over and finish frying until golden brown.

4

Top with grated cheese and serve warm.

Egg-In-Pepper

Fun food is what kids love, and this is exactly that kind of food. It can't get easier than this!

Serves: 2

Ingredients:

- 2 thick slices red bell pepper
- 2 eggs
- Salt, pepper to taste
- 2 tablespoons olive oil

Directions:

1

Heat the olive oil in a skillet.

2

Place the bell pepper slices in the pan, then crack open the eggs and drop them in the center of each slice.

3

Gently press the slice into the oil to seal the edges, then fry the egg as you normally would.

4

Serve right away.

Tomato and Avocado Sandwich

Avocado is a great addition to your child's diet because it is rich in good fats, which are so needed for good development of the brain. Plus, it has a mild taste, and it can be seasoned or combined with practically anything.

Serves: 4

Ingredients:

- 8 slices white sandwich bread
- 4 lettuce leaves
- 4 slices tomato
- 1 ripe avocado, peeled and sliced
- Salt, pepper to taste

Directions:

1

Place 4 of the sandwich bread slices on your working surface.

2

Top each slice with lettuce, tomatoes, and avocado, then season with salt and pepper.

3

Cover with the other 4 slices of bread to form the sandwiches and serve fresh.

Flat Bread Skillet Pizza

Pizza can be quite time consuming when made from scratch, but this version is quick, just as delicious, and uses common ingredients. Just pick your toppings, and you're good to go.

Serves: 2

Ingredients:

- 2 flat breads
- 2 ripe tomatoes, sliced
- ½ cup tomato sauce
- 1 cup shredded mozzarella

Directions:

1
Spread tomato sauce over the two flat breads.

2
Top with tomato slices and mozzarella, then place the flatbreads in a preheated skillet.

3
Cover with a lid and cook 5-10 minutes.

4
Serve the flat bread pizza warm and fresh.

Poached Tofu with Tomato Sauce

Tofu is a great source of protein, and it should be included in your family's diet. You will love the tenderness and juiciness of this dish.

Serves: 4

Ingredients:

- 4 thick slices of firm tofu
- 1 cup canned diced tomatoes
- 1 cup tomato puree
- 1 bay leaf
- 2 garlic cloves, crushed
- 2 tablespoons olive oil
- Salt, pepper to taste

Directions:

1
Combine the tomatoes and tomato puree in a saucepan. Add the bay leaf, garlic, and olive oil; salt and pepper to taste and bring to a boil.

2
Place the tofu slices into the boiling sauce and cook for 10-15 minutes.

3
Serve the tofu right away, topped with plenty of sauce.

Cilantro Tofu Fillets

Don't underestimate tofu! It's a delicious substitute for meat, and it tastes great if cooked properly.

Serves: 4

Ingredients:

- 4 thick tofu slices
- 4 tablespoons vegetable oil
- ¼ cup chicken stock
- 1 tablespoon lemon juice
- 2 tablespoons chopped cilantro
- Salt, pepper to taste

Directions:

1
Heat the oil in a skillet and add the tofu slices. Cook them on both sides until golden brown, then pour in the stock.

2
Turn the heat on high and cook for 5-10 minutes.

3
Just before removing from heat, add the lemon juice and cilantro.

4
Serve the tofu right away.

Quick Lettuce Wraps

Kids love wraps, but why not make your own at home, with fresh ingredients that are much healthier and definitely delicious? You can even get them involved in the process.

Serves: 4

Ingredients:

- 4 large lettuce leaves
- 1 ripe avocado, peeled and sliced
- 2 ripe tomatoes, sliced
- 1 cucumber, sliced
- 1 bunch chopped parsley
- ¼ cup Greek style yogurt
- Salt, pepper to taste

Directions:

1. Lay the lettuce leaves flat on your working surface.
2. Place the avocado in the center and top it with tomatoes, cucumber, parsley, and yogurt.
3. Season with salt and pepper, then tightly wrap the lettuce.
4. Serve right away.

Cheesy Grits

Grits are easy to cook and kids usually love them, but this is not the usual version. It has plenty of cheese to create a dish that really stands out.

Serves: 2-4

Ingredients:

- 1 cup quick cooking grits
- 2 cups hot vegetable stock
- 2 cups hot water
- 1 cup grated cheddar
- ½ cup grated Parmesan
- 1 pinch nutmeg
- Salt, pepper to taste

Directions:

1
Combine the stock with the water in a saucepan. Stir in the grits and cook for 10 minutes on medium heat.

2
Season with salt and pepper, then add the nutmeg.

3
Remove from heat and stir in the grated cheese.

4
Spoon the grits into serving bowls and serve warm while the cheese is melting.

Cheesy Mushrooms

Cheese and mushrooms come together in this quick meal to create a dish that is both rich and flavorful. Imagine all that melted cheese oozing out with every bite! Delicious!

Serves: 4

Ingredients:

- 4 Portobello mushrooms
- 1 cup grated cheddar
- 1 cup shredded mozzarella
- ½ teaspoon dried thyme

Directions:

1

Place the mushrooms on a baking tray.

2

Top with cheddar and mozzarella, then sprinkle with dried thyme.

3

Bake the mushrooms at 400°F for 10-15 minutes.

4

Serve the mushrooms right away.

Ricotta Cheese Fritters

These fritters can become either a quick snack or dessert if you serve them with fruit jam or a savory sauce. That's how versatile they are!

Serves: 2-4

Ingredients:

- 2 eggs
- 3 cups fresh ricotta
- 1 pinch nutmeg
- ¼ cup grated Parmesan
- 1 tablespoon olive oil
- 1 pinch of salt
- ½ cup vegetable oil for frying

Directions:

1

Mix the eggs and ricotta, then stir in the nutmeg, Parmesan, olive oil, and salt.

2

Heat the vegetable oil in a skillet and drop spoonfuls of batter into the hot oil.

3

Fry the fritters on both sides until golden brown.

4

Serve the fritters with yogurt or your sauce of choice.

Fried Rice with Tomato

Fried rice is quick, but adding tomatoes enhances the flavor and yields a juicy, moist rice, perfect for lunch or dinner.

Serves: 2-4

Ingredients:

- 2 cups cooked white rice
- 2 green onions, chopped
- 2 garlic cloves, chopped
- ½ red pepper, sliced
- 1 cup green peas
- 2 tablespoons olive oil
- 1 teaspoon soy sauce
- 1 teaspoon fish sauce
- 3 eggs, beaten
- 1 ripe tomato, diced
- Salt, pepper to taste

Directions:

1. Heat the olive oil in a skillet and stir in the green onions and garlic. Sauté for 1 minute, then add the red pepper, green peas, and rice.
2. Sauté for 2 more minutes.
3. Mix the eggs with the tomato, soy sauce, and fish sauce, then pour the eggs over the rice.
4. Mix well until the eggs are set.
5. Serve warm.

Creamy Corn Soup

Corn is nutritious, loaded with fiber, and has a rather sweet taste, not to mention that children think corn is fun and delicious.

Serves: 2-4

Ingredients:

- 1 can sweet corn, drained
- 2 cups vegetable stock
- 2 green onions, chopped
- 2 garlic cloves, chopped
- 2 tablespoons olive oil
- 1 cup coconut milk
- Salt, pepper to taste
- 2 tablespoons chopped cilantro

Directions:

1

Heat the olive oil in a soup pot, then stir in the green onions and garlic. Sauté for 2 minutes.

2

Add the corn, vegetable stock, and coconut milk and cook for 10 minutes.

3

Season with salt and pepper to taste, then remove from heat.

4

Add the cilantro and serve the soup warm.

Quick Burritos

Kids are huge fans of burritos. These are quick and easy to make as well as delicious and rich.

Serves: 4

Ingredients:

- 1 can black beans, drained
- 4 green onions, chopped
- 2 garlic cloves, chopped
- ½ teaspoon smoked paprika
- 2 tablespoons olive oil
- Salt, pepper to taste
- 4 flour tortillas

Directions:

1
Heat the olive oil in a skillet and stir in the garlic and green onions.

2
Stir in the beans and paprika and add salt and pepper to taste.

3
Cook the beans for 10 minutes.

4
Spoon the beans into the 4 tortillas and wrap them tightly.

5
Serve fresh.

Italian Grilled Sandwich

Who doesn't love sandwiches? Kids especially do! They love to grab a sandwich and get back to playing or studying, and this one is nutritious and flavorful, absolutely delicious.

Serves: 2

Ingredients:

- 4 slices white bread
- 2 tablespoons Italian pesto
- 2 slices mozzarella cheese
- 2 slices tomatoes

Directions:

1

Place 2 slices bread on your working surface and spread the pesto on both.

2

Top with cheese and tomatoes, then cover with the other two bread slices.

3

Heat a grill pan over medium heat and place the sandwiches into the pan.

4

Cook on both sides until the cheese is melted.

5

Serve the sandwiches warm.

Guacamole Bites

Avocado is an amazing fruit—rich, creamy, and delicate; and guacamole is all about avocado, but it is great combined with tomatoes, garlic, and lemon juice, then served on pieces of toasted bread.

Serves: 2-4

Ingredients:

- 1 ripe avocado, peeled
- 1 garlic clove, minced
- 2 ripe tomatoes, diced
- ¼ cup chopped parsley
- 2 tablespoons chopped cilantro
- 2 tablespoons lemon juice
- Salt, pepper to taste
- 4-6 slices white bread, toasted and cubed

Directions:

1

Mash the avocado with a fork, then stir in the garlic, tomatoes, parsley, cilantro, and lemon juice.

2

Season with salt and pepper, then top the bread pieces with the guacamole.

3

Serve fresh.

Summer Pasta Salad

Fresh, light, and easy to make, this salad is a huge hit with the entire family because it can be made with their favorite veggies. Plus, if you use kids' pasta, it will also turn into a fun dish since pasta for children has various fun shapes.

Serves: 2-4

Ingredients:

- 10 oz. cooked pasta, drained
- 1 cucumber, sliced
- 1 red onion, sliced
- 2 tomatoes, sliced
- 4 basil leaves, chopped
- 1 pound shredded mozzarella cheese
- ¼ cup olive oil
- ½ lemon, juiced
- Salt, pepper to taste

Directions:

1
Combine the pasta with the vegetables, then add the basil and mozzarella.

2
Drizzle with lemon juice and olive oil, then season with salt and pepper to taste.

3
Serve the salad fresh or refrigerate for up to a few hours in an airtight container in the fridge.

Caramel Apples

Caramel apples are such a fun treat, even for children! The ingredient list is so short, and yet, the outcome is so delicious!

Serves: 4

Ingredients:

- 1 cup brown sugar
- 4 small green apples
- 4 wooden skewers
- ½ cup chopped walnuts

Directions:

1

Melt the brown sugar in a saucepan.

2

Place the apples on skewers, then dip each apple into the caramel, coating it as much as possible.

3

Roll the apples through chopped walnuts and place them on a baking sheet.

4

Let them set and cool, then serve.

Tempeh Reuben Sandwich

The Reuben sandwich is a classic that combines various ingredients with sauerkraut, which is very healthy and juicy. This particular recipe uses tempeh to add a boost of protein, and it tastes great—so just try it.

Serves: 4

Ingredients:

- 8 slices whole wheat bread
- 2 cups sauerkraut, drained
- 4 slices tempeh
- 4 slices Swiss cheese
- 2 tablespoons mustard

Directions:

1. Take 4 slices of bread and place them on your working surface.
2. Spread mustard on each slice, then top with tempeh, cheese, and sauerkraut.
3. Cover with the remaining bread to form the sandwiches, then place each on a preheated grill pan and cook just a few minutes until the cheese is melted.
4. Serve fresh and warm.

Crunchy Zucchini Sauté

Don't underestimate zucchinis. They may have a high water content, but they are also loaded with minerals and vitamins. Plus, they are easy and quick to cook and very easy to season as well.

Serves: 2-4

Ingredients:

- 2 zucchinis, sliced
- 3 tablespoons olive oil
- 2 garlic cloves, chopped
- ¼ cup chopped pecans
- 2 tablespoons balsamic vinegar
- Salt, pepper to taste

Directions:

1. Heat the oil in a skillet and stir in the garlic.
2. Sauté for 1 minute, then add the zucchini.
3. Cook on high heat for 10 minutes, then add the pecans and cook 2 more minutes.
4. Season with salt and pepper to taste; remove from heat.
5. Add the balsamic vinegar and serve right away.

Greek Salad

Fresh vegetables are healthy and nutritious for the entire family, but especially for kids. They will benefit from all those vitamins, antioxidants, and fibers, for sure.

Serves: 2-4

Ingredients:

- 1 ½ pounds ripe tomatoes
- 1 cucumber, sliced
- 1 avocado, peeled and cubed
- 2 tablespoons balsamic vinegar
- 2 tablespoons olive oil
- 4 oz. feta cheese, cubed
- 4 basil leaves, chopped
- ¼ cup chopped parsley
- Salt, pepper to taste

Directions:

1
Combine the tomatoes with the cucumber, avocado, feta cheese, basil, and parsley.

2
Stir in the balsamic vinegar and olive oil, then season with salt and pepper.

3
Serve the salad as fresh as possible.

Spinach and Broccoli Salad

I know that this salad has two main ingredients that kids tend to avoid, but if that is the case with your kids, don't give up. As long as they are willing to taste, you have a good chance to get them to eat it because this salad is truly delicious and so colorful.

Serves: 2-4

Ingredients:

- 4 cups baby spinach
- 1 cucumber, sliced
- 1 cup chopped broccoli florets
- 2 green onions, chopped
- ¼ cup Greek style yogurt
- 2 garlic cloves, minced
- 4 tablespoons olive oil
- 2 tablespoons lemon juice
- Salt, pepper to taste

Directions:

1
Combine the spinach, cucumber, broccoli, and green onions in a bowl.

2
In a different bowl, combine the yogurt with the garlic, olive oil, lemon juice, salt, and pepper; mix well.

3
Drizzle the dressing over the salad and serve it as fresh as possible.

Rice and Egg Salad

Rice is nutritious and delicious in most combinations, but this recipe is creamy and so rich. Your kids will love it!

Serves: 2-4

Ingredients:

- 2 cups cooked rice
- 4 hard-boiled eggs, cubed
- 2 green onions, chopped
- 1 red bell pepper, cored and diced
- Salt, pepper to taste
- 2 tablespoons lemon juice

Directions:

1

Mix the cooked rice with the hard-boiled eggs, green onions, and bell pepper in a bowl.

2

Season with salt and pepper to taste, then add the lemon juice.

3

Serve the salad as fresh as possible.

Tortillas Filled with Cream Cheese

Tortillas are very easy to incorporate into your children's diet because they can literally be combined with any vegetables or cheese. This recipe brings out a combination that you will love: cream cheese, herbs, and tomatoes.

Serves: 4

Ingredients:

- 1 cup cream cheese
- 2 tablespoons chopped dill
- 2 tablespoons chopped parsley
- Salt, pepper to taste
- 4 tortillas
- 2 ripe tomatoes, sliced
- ½ head lettuce, shredded
- 2 tablespoons olive oil

Directions:

1

Combine the cream cheese with the dill and parsley, then season with salt and pepper to taste.

2

Spread the cream cheese over the 4 tortillas, then top with shredded lettuce and tomatoes.

3

Drizzle with a touch of olive oil.

4

Wrap the tortillas tightly and serve them right away.

Sweet Potato Thyme Hash

Sweet potatoes are kids' favorites due to their sweet flavor, but they taste great combined with thyme; you have to try it. The thyme just enhances their flavor even more.

Serves: 2-4

Ingredients:

- 4 sweet potatoes, peeled and diced
- 1 garlic clove, chopped
- 4 tablespoons olive oil
- ½ teaspoon sweet paprika
- 1 pinch smoked paprika
- 1 teaspoon dried thyme
- Salt, pepper to taste

Directions:

1

Heat the olive oil in a skillet and stir in the garlic.

2

Sauté for 1 minute, then add the sweet potatoes.

3

Cook the potatoes on medium heat for 10-12 minutes, stirring often.

4

Add the paprika and thyme, then season with salt and pepper.

5

Serve the hashed potatoes right away.

Potato Pancakes

Potatoes are amazing ingredients due to their versatility. These potato pancakes are moist and delicious, perfect as a little snack for your kids and great for leftovers—if you have any.

Serves: 2-4

Ingredients:

- 2 cups mashed potatoes
- 1 egg
- ¼ cup grated cheddar cheese
- 1 tablespoon chopped parsley
- Salt, pepper to taste
- ¼ cup vegetable oil for frying

Directions:

1
Combine the mashed potatoes with the egg, cheese, parsley, salt, and pepper in a bowl.

2
Heat the oil in a frying pan and drop spoonfuls of the potato batter into the hot oil.

3
Fry on both sides until golden brown; remove the pancakes from the oil and place on paper towels to absorb excess oil.

4
Serve them fresh, warm or cool.

Quick and Easy Recipes for Romantic Meals

Love is an amazing thing to have in one's life! It makes us better people, it makes us happy, it gives us stability, and it makes us creative and kind. Love makes us want to do lovely, romantic things for each other, and a romantic meal is at the top of the list for sure. After all, food is one of the most important things in life, and it is normal to want to surprise and impress your loved one with a delicious meal. No wonder that people say love goes through the stomach first.

But what do you do when you don't have time for cooking? The answer is simple! You open this book and read this full chapter. It has 30 recipes designed just for you and your loved one. Each and every one of these recipes are delicious, fail-proof, and have so much flavor that no one can resist them. And they only take 15 minutes to make. What more can you ask for?

Granola Parfait

Breakfast is the most important meal of the day, like it or not! This granola parfait is perfect to offer you a great start to the day.

Serves: 2-4

Ingredients:

- 1 cup granola
- ½ cup chopped almonds
- 2 cups Greek style yogurt
- 2 tablespoons honey
- 1 cup mixed berries
- 2 mint leaves, chopped

Directions:

1

Combine the yogurt with the honey and mint.

2

Layer the granola, almonds, yogurt, and berries in serving glasses or bowls.

3

Serve fresh or store them in the fridge for up to a few hours.

Nutella French Toast

This is not your usual French toast recipe! Nutella is delicious anyway, but imagine two slices of bread filled with plenty of Nutella, then fried until the Nutella is melted and oozing out with each bite.

Serves: 4

Ingredients:

- 8 slices white bread
- 1 cup Nutella
- 4 eggs, beaten
- 2 tablespoons heavy cream
- 1 teaspoon vanilla extract
- 4 tablespoons vegetable oil

Directions:

1

Combine the eggs with the heavy cream and vanilla.

2

Spread the Nutella on all slices of bread, then glue them together two by two.

3

Heat the oil in a frying pan.

4

Dip the Nutella sandwiches in the egg mixture and drop them into the hot oil.

5

Fry them on both sides until golden brown.

6

Serve right away.

Pesto Omelet

Don't underestimate the classic, common omelet! Making one that actually tastes good is not that easy, but this recipe is sure to be a hit with your loved one due to its intense taste.

Serves: 2-4

Ingredients:

- 5 eggs, beaten
- 2 tablespoons pesto
- 2 ripe tomatoes, diced
- Salt, pepper to taste
- 3 tablespoons olive oil

Directions:

1
Heat the olive oil in a skillet.

2
Mix the eggs with the pesto, tomatoes, salt, and pepper, then pour the mixture into the skillet.

3
Cook the omelet on one side until golden brown, then flip it over and finish cooking.

4
Serve warm.

Nutella Trifle

Trifle is a creamy, rich dessert that takes little time to make, and it is delicious. This particular recipe uses Nutella, heavy cream, and crushed cookies to create a dessert that your better half will love. You can make it even one day ahead.

Serves: 2

Ingredients:

- ½ cup Nutella
- 1 cup heavy cream, whipped
- 1 cup crushed sugar cookies
- 1 cup sliced strawberries

Directions:

1

Combine the Nutella with the whipped cream in a bowl.

2

Layer the crushed cookies, strawberries, and Nutella into 2 serving glasses.

3

with strawberry slices and serve right away.

Caprese Salad

Simplicity is the key to impressing your loved one. It doesn't have to be a complicated dish to show him or her your love as long as you keep the ingredients fresh and the flavor combinations basic. This salad is one of the best choices because it combines ingredients that most people love. It also has a delicate flavor display and plenty of nutrients, if it matters.

Serves: 2-4

Ingredients:

- 4 ripe tomatoes, sliced
- 4 oz. mozzarella, sliced
- 4 tablespoons olive oil
- Salt, pepper to taste
- 6 basil leaves, shredded

Directions:

1

Layer the tomato and mozzarella slices on a platter.

2

Season with salt and pepper and drizzle with olive oil.

3

Top with basil and serve the salad as fresh as possible.

Straciatella Yogurt Mousse

You don't need any special skills to make this delicate and delicious mousse. It is both delicious and healthy, but most of all, it takes less than 15 minutes to make.

Serves: 4

Ingredients:

- 2 cups Greek style yogurt
- 1 ½ cups heavy cream, whipped
- ½ cup chocolate shavings
- 4 tablespoons powdered sugar
- 1 teaspoon vanilla extract

Directions:

1

Combine the yogurt with the chocolate shavings, sugar, and vanilla.

2

Fold in the whipped cream, then spoon the mousse into serving glasses.

3

Serve right away or refrigerate for a few hours before serving.

Grilled Tofu Steak with Kale Sauté

Tofu is a great source of protein, and it tastes great if you cook it properly. The simplest and most delicious way is definitely grilling. This recipe is a winner!

Serves: 4

Ingredients:

Grilled tofu –
- 4 thick slices firm tofu
- 2 tablespoons pesto
- 2 tablespoons lemon juice
- 2 tablespoons olive oil
- 2 garlic cloves, chopped
- 1 pinch chili flakes

Kale sauté –
- 1 bunch kale
- 2 tablespoons olive oil
- 2 garlic cloves, chopped
- 1 pinch cumin powder

Directions:

1

Combine the pesto, lemon juice, olive oil, garlic, and chili in a bowl.

2

Add the tofu slices and let them marinade for a few hours—overnight, if possible.

3

Heat a grill pan over medium heat and place the tofu slices on the grill. Cook them until browned on both sides.

5

To make the kale, heat the olive oil in a skillet. You can do the sauté while the tofu is grilling.

6

Stir in the garlic and cook 30 seconds, then add the kale and cumin.

7

Sauté for 10 minutes on medium heat. Place the kale on a plate and arrange a slice of grilled tofu on top. Serve right away.

Tomato and Basil Sauce Pasta

This dish may be simple, but it won't fail to impress! It uses ingredients that are easy to find all year around, so you can make this delicacy at any time.

Serves: 2-4

Ingredients:

- 10 oz. spaghetti
- 1 can diced tomatoes
- ¼ cup white wine
- 1 bay leaf
- 2 garlic cloves, chopped
- ½ shallot, chopped
- 4 tablespoons olive oil
- ½ cup black olives
- Salt, pepper to taste
- 4 basil leaves, chopped

Directions:

1

Pour a few cups of water into a large pot and bring it to a boil with a pinch of salt.

2

Throw in the spaghetti and cook until al dente.

3

In the meantime, heat the oil in a skillet and stir in the garlic and shallot. Sauté for 2 minutes, then add the tomatoes and wine.

4

Season with salt and pepper and cook the sauce for 5-10 minutes on medium heat.

5

Drain the pasta and place it into the skillet.

6

Add the olives, mix a few times, then remove from heat and serve topped with basil.

Spinach and Strawberry Balsamic Salad

As unusual as it sounds, this combination is actually delicious. The spinach is fresh and sweet, the strawberries are slightly tangy, and the balsamic is earthy. The final salad is well balanced, tastes great, and has a beautiful color.

Serves: 2-4

Ingredients:

- 1 pound fresh spinach
- 1 cup fresh strawberries, halved
- 4 tablespoons balsamic vinegar
- 2 tablespoons olive oil
- Salt, pepper to taste

Directions:

1

Combine the vinegar with the olive oil, salt, and pepper in a bowl.

2

Place the spinach on a platter. Top with strawberries, then drizzle with the balsamic dressing.

3

Serve the salad as fresh as possible.

Roasted Bell Pepper Soup

Creamy and smoky, this soup is a real delight for your taste buds. You and your other half will love not only the consistency but also the intense aroma and the delicate spice.

Serves: 2-4

Ingredients:

- 1 jar roasted red bell peppers, drained
- 2 garlic cloves, chopped
- 1 shallot, chopped
- 3 tablespoons olive oil
- ½ teaspoon cumin powder
- 3 cups vegetable stock
- Salt, pepper to taste
- Sour cream to serve

Directions:

1

Heat the olive oil in a soup pot.

2

Stir in the garlic and shallot and sauté 2 minutes, then add the bell peppers, cumin powder, and stock.

3

Cook the soup for 10 minutes on high heat.

4

Puree the soup with an immersion blender, then season with salt and pepper to taste.

5

Pour the soup in bowls and top with a dollop of sour cream before serving.

Chili Pecorino Spaghetti

The ingredient list is incredibly short, but the outcome is delicious. You won't believe that just a few common ingredients can yield such a delicious dish. Plus, don't forget that chili is an aphrodisiac.

Serves: 2-4

Ingredients:

- 10 oz. spaghetti
- ¼ cup olive oil
- 1 teaspoon chili flakes
- 1 garlic clove, chopped
- 1 ½ cups grated Pecorino cheese

Directions:

1. Pour a few cups of water into a pot and bring it to a boil with a pinch of salt.
2. Throw in the spaghetti and cook until al dente, not more than 10 minutes.
3. In the meantime, heat the oil in a skillet and stir in the garlic and chili flakes.
4. Sauté 30 seconds, then add the pasta.
5. Mix a few times and remove from heat.
6. Transfer to platters and top with grated cheese just before serving.

Spiced Sautéed Mushrooms

Mushrooms are earthy and nutritious but also quick and easy to cook. A sauté is the simplest way to cook them, but simple means delicious in this case. Plus, the spices really make them shine.

Serves: 2-4

Ingredients:

- 1 ½ pounds mushrooms, sliced
- 1 pinch chili flakes
- ½ teaspoon cumin powder
- 1 pinch nutmeg
- 2 garlic cloves, chopped
- 4 tablespoons canola oil
- Salt, pepper to taste

Directions:

1
Heat the olive oil in a skillet and stir in the garlic.

2
Sauté 30 seconds, then add the mushrooms.

3
Cook them on high heat for 10 minutes.

4
Season with salt and pepper, then add the cumin, chili flakes, and nutmeg.

5
Cook 1 more minute, then remove from heat.

6
Serve warm and fresh.

Sage Gnocchi

Gnocchi can be found on the fresh pasta island in most supermarkets, and they are amazing because they don't take much time to make. This recipe combines them with sage, which is a real classic, but it can proudly be served at a romantic dinner with a glass of good white wine.

Serves: 2-4

Ingredients:

- 1 pound fresh gnocchi
- 3 tablespoons butter
- 4 tablespoons white wine
- 4 sage leaves
- Salt, pepper to taste

Directions:

1

Melt the butter in a skillet.

2

Add the white wine and sage, then throw in the gnocchi.

3

Season with salt and pepper and cook them for 10 minutes on medium heat.

4

Serve warm with a glass of white wine.

Lentil and Cucumber Salad

If you're looking for a one-of-a-kind salad, this is the one! The lentils are filling and rich, and the cucumber is fresh. The final result is a refreshing and delicious salad that will please even the pickiest eater.

Serves: 2-4

Ingredients:
- 1 can lentils, drained
- 2 green onions, chopped
- 2 tomatoes, cubed
- 2 cucumbers, sliced
- ½ cup chopped parsley
- ½ cup chopped cilantro
- ½ red pepper, sliced
- 1 teaspoon capers, chopped
- Salt, pepper to taste
- ½ lemon, juiced
- 2 tablespoons olive oil

Directions:

1
Combine the lentils with the green onions, tomatoes, cucumbers, capers, red pepper, parsley, and cilantro.

2
Season with salt and pepper to taste.

3
Stir in the lemon juice and olive oil and mix gently.

4
Serve the salad as fresh as possible.

Spinach and Ricotta Raw Lasagna

Forget the meat sauce for lasagna. This recipe is vegetarian, but just as delicious and rich. You will love how all the different layers come together to create a dish that will stand out.

Serves: 6-8

Ingredients:

- 10 oz. fresh ricotta
- ¼ cup chopped parsley
- 2 tablespoons chopped basil
- 2 zucchinis, sliced lengthwise
- 4 cups spinach
- 2 garlic cloves, chopped
- 2 tablespoons olive oil
- Salt, pepper to taste

Directions:

1
Heat the olive oil in a skillet and stir in the garlic. Sauté for 30 seconds, then add the spinach.

2
Season with salt and pepper and sauté for 5 minutes.

3
Combine the ricotta with the parsley and basil in another bowl. Add salt and pepper to taste.

4
Layer the zucchini slices, ricotta, and sautéed spinach in a deep bowl.

5
Serve the lasagna right away.

Shakshouka – Tomato Poached Eggs

Shakshouka is a dish that has Oriental origins. It is fresh, rich, spicy, and absolutely delicious. Surprise your loved one with this, and he or she will be pleased.

Serves: 2

Ingredients:

- 2 cups canned diced tomatoes
- ½ cup tomato puree
- 1 shallot, chopped
- 2 garlic cloves, chopped
- 4 tablespoons olive oil
- 4 eggs
- Salt, pepper to taste
- ½ teaspoon cumin powder
- ½ teaspoon garam masala

Directions:

1
Heat the oil in a heavy frying pan and stir in the shallot and garlic.

2
Sauté for 2 minutes, then add the tomatoes, tomato puree, garlic, cumin, and garam masala.

3
Bring the sauce to a boil and cook it for 10 minutes, adding salt and pepper to taste.

4
Crack open the eggs and drop them into the hot sauce.

5
Cover with a lid and cook just until the eggs are set.

6
Serve warm.

Three-Cheese Pasta

This cheesy sauce is more than delicious. It will flood your mouth and taste buds with deliciousness, creaminess, and so much flavor that you and you loved one will both get hooked!

Serves: 2-4

Ingredients:
- 10 oz. short pasta
- 1 cup grated cheddar
- 1 cup shredded mozzarella
- ½ cup grated Parmesan
- 1 pinch nutmeg
- 1 pinch black pepper
- 2 cups hot milk
- 2 tablespoons butter
- 2 tablespoons all-purpose flour

Directions:

1

Pour a few cups of water in a large pot with a pinch of salt and bring it to a boil.

2

Throw in the pasta and cook it until al dente, not more than 10 minutes.

3

In the meantime, melt the butter in a heavy saucepan and stir in the flour.

4

Sauté for 1 minute, then pour in the milk.

5

Cook on medium heat until thickened, stirring often.

6

Add nutmeg, black pepper, and the three cheeses; mix well.

7

Drain the pasta and mix it into the sauce.

8

Serve warm.

Cheese-Filled Croissants

Sweet and salty are two of the main tastes, and they can be combined in the same dish if you balance them well. For instance, a sweet croissant and a salty cheese have the right amount of salty and sweet to yield an amazing snack or meal for two.

Serves: 2

Ingredients:

- 2 butter croissants
- 1 cup grated cheddar cheese
- 1 pinch nutmeg

Directions:

1

Slice the croissants lengthwise.

2

Fill them with grated cheese and sprinkle with a pinch of nutmeg.

3

Microwave the croissants for 2 minutes, then serve.

Battered Tofu

Tofu tastes great in this recipe because once fried, the batter traps in the moisture, and the final result is a moist, fragrant, and delicious slice of tofu that can then be served with your favorite side dish.

Serves: 2

Ingredients:

- 2 thick slices firm tofu
- ½ cup all-purpose flour
- ¼ cup beer
- ¼ cup ice cold water
- 1 pinch salt
- 1 pinch dried basil
- 1 cup vegetable oil for frying

Directions:

1
Combine the flour with the beer, water, salt, and basil in a bowl and mix well.

2
Heat the oil in a deep saucepan.

3
Dip the tofu slices into the batter, then drop each slice into the hot oil.

4
Fry the tofu until golden brown on all sides.

5
Serve with your favorite side dish.

Tofu Piccata

Piccata is a classic Italian dish usually made with chicken, but this version that uses tofu is just as delicious! Your loved one will appreciate the delicate sauce and the tenderness of the tofu.

Serves: 4

Ingredients:

- 4 slices firm tofu
- 2 tablespoons all-purpose flour
- 4 tablespoons olive oil
- 2 garlic cloves, chopped
- ½ cup white wine
- ½ lemon, juiced
- 1 teaspoon capers, chopped
- Salt, pepper to taste

Directions:

1. Heat the olive oil in a skillet.
2. Roll the tofu slices through the flour and place them into the skillet.
3. Quickly fry them on high heat, then add the garlic.
4. Sauté for 30 seconds, then pour in the white wine and lemon juice.
5. Add the capers and cook over medium heat for 10 minutes.
6. Adjust the taste with salt and pepper and serve the tofu right away.

Chocolate Fondue

This is the perfect dessert for two, don't you agree?! Imagine those fruits dipped into melted chocolate! It's a delicacy, and you can't go wrong with it.

Serves: 2

Ingredients:

- 8 oz. dark chocolate
- 4 oz. heavy cream
- 2 oranges, sliced
- 2 ripe bananas, sliced
- 4 oz. fresh strawberries

Directions:

1

Place the chocolate in a heatproof bowl. Add the heavy cream and microwave for 30 seconds at a time until the chocolate is melted and the cream is smooth.

2

Spoon into an elegant serving bowl.

3

To serve, use skewers and dip the fruits into the melted chocolate.

Lemon Flavored Roasted Asparagus

Asparagus is a delicate vegetable, and it truly shines when combined with lemon because the lemon adds enough freshness to enhance its flavor.

Serves: 2

Ingredients:

- 1 pound fresh asparagus, trimmed
- ½ lemon, juiced
- ¼ cup olive oil
- Salt, pepper to taste
- 1 pinch chili flakes

Directions:

1

Mix the lemon juice with the olive oil.

2

Add salt and pepper to taste along with a pinch of chili flakes.

3

Brush the asparagus with the mixture and place it on a baking tray.

4

Roast the asparagus on your highest temperature for 10-15 minutes.

5

Serve fresh.

Sweet and Spicy Tofu Stir Fry

Stir fry is quick and delicious, but this tofu version goes beyond expectations by combining the salty tofu with spices and bokchoy. Simple and delicious!

Serves: 2-4

Ingredients:

- 2 tablespoons canola oil
- 8 oz. firm tofu, cubed
- 2 green onions, chopped
- 1 teaspoon dried thyme
- 1 pinch dried sage
- 1 pinch cayenne pepper
- ¼ cup vegetable stock
- 2 bokchoy, chopped
- 1 tablespoon soy sauce

Directions:

1

Heat the canola oil in a wok.

2

Stir in the tofu and cook for 5 minutes.

3

Throw in the green onions, thyme, sage, cayenne pepper, and stock.

4

Keep cooking on high heat for 5 more minutes, then add the bokchoy and soy sauce.

5

Sauté 2 more minutes, then remove from heat and serve.

Tofu and Ginger Soup

This soup is a real delight if you love Asian flavors. Tofu, ginger, and soy sauce are some of the main ingredients, and the final result is absolutely delicious.

Serves: 2-4

Ingredients:

- 2 tablespoons canola oil
- ½ pound tofu, cubed
- 1-inch piece of ginger
- 2 garlic cloves, chopped
- 3 cups vegetable stock
- 1 tablespoon soy sauce
- ½ red pepper, sliced
- 1 bokchoy, shredded

Directions:

1

Heat the canola oil in a soup pot and stir in the tofu. Sauté for 2 minutes, then add the ginger, garlic, stock, and soy sauce, as well as the red pepper.

2

Bring to a boil and add the bokchoy.

3

Cook the soup for 10 minutes.

4

Serve fresh and warm.

Tofu au Vin

This is a very quick version of tofu and wine sauce, and it is delicious. Tofu is usually very mild, but in this combination, it tastes great. You will love it!

Serves: 2-4

Ingredients:

- 8 oz. firm tofu, cubed
- 2 tablespoons canola oil
- 2 tablespoons balsamic vinegar
- 1 pinch cayenne pepper
- ½ cup canned pearl onions, drained
- 2 garlic cloves, chopped
- 5 oz. mushrooms, sliced
- ½ cup red wine
- ½ cup vegetable stock
- Salt, pepper to taste

Directions:

1

Heat the oil in a heavy saucepan and stir in the tofu. Sauté for 2 minutes, then add the rest of the ingredients.

2

Turn the heat on high and cook the tofu for 10 minutes until the sauce begins to thicken.

3

Season with salt and pepper and serve warm.

Poached Brussels Sprouts with Parmesan Topping

Don't underestimate Brussels sprouts. If you combine them with the right ingredients, they turn into real delicacies, and Parmesan is one of those ingredients!

Serves: 2-4

Ingredients:

- 4 cups water
- 2 garlic cloves, crushed
- 1 pound Brussels sprouts, halved
- ½ lemon, juiced
- 4 tablespoons olive oil
- 1 teaspoon lemon zest
- 1 cup grated Parmesan
- Salt, pepper to taste

Directions:

1. Pour the water in a pot and bring to a boil with a pinch of salt.
2. Throw in the sprouts and cook for 10 minutes. Drain them and set aside in a bowl.
3. Combine the lemon juice, olive oil, lemon zest, salt and pepper in a small bowl.
4. Pour the dressing over the sprouts and mix gently.
5. Top with grated Parmesan and serve fresh.

Caramel Pears

How delicate this dish is! Pears are juicy and have an earthy aroma that pairs wonderfully with the caramel. What you get is a dessert like no other—creamy, rich, and fragrant!

Serves: 4

Ingredients:

- 4 ripe pears, peeled and sliced
- ½ cup brown sugar
- ½ cup water
- 2 tablespoons butter
- 1 pinch salt
- 4 scoops vanilla ice cream to serve

Directions:

1

Melt the brown sugar in a skillet.

2

Add the butter, then pour in the water and add a pinch of salt.

3

Place the pear slices into the skillet and cook for 6-8 minutes, flipping them over.

4

They don't need much time to cook because they have to remain a bit crunchy.

5

Serve the pears topped with vanilla ice cream.

Cheesecake Bites

You don't need to spend over an hour to be able to enjoy a rich and delicious cheesecake. This is a shortcut to getting the same taste but much quicker, and it's great if you or your loved one likes cheesecake.

Serves: 2

Ingredients:

- 8 whole wheat crackers
- ½ cup cream cheese
- 2 tablespoons honey
- 1 teaspoon lemon zest
- ½ teaspoon vanilla extract
- 1 cup strawberries, sliced

Directions:

1

Combine the cream cheese with honey, lemon zest, and vanilla.

2

Spread the cream cheese over crackers and top with fresh strawberries.

3

Serve right away.

Minty Fruit Salad Cups

Fruit salad is a hit in any situation, including a dinner for two, but this version adds a touch of mint, creating a truly refreshing and fragrant salad for those summer days.

Serves: 2

Ingredients:

- 2 oranges, cut into segments
- 2 kiwi fruits, peeled and sliced
- 1 ripe pear, peeled and cubed
- 1 apple, peeled and cubed
- ½ cup mango cubes
- 4 mint leaves
- 2 tablespoons honey
- 1 tablespoon light rum
- 1 cup whipped cream

Directions:

1

Combine all the fruits in a bowl.

2

Stir in the chopped mint, honey, and light rum.

3

Spoon the salad into individual serving glasses or bowls and top them with whipped cream.

4

Serve fresh.

Grilled Peaches with Raspberry Sorbet

Grilling peaches enhances their taste, and it also adds a delicate smoky flavor that tastes great in this combination. The peaches turn tender and juicy, and they get so much flavor that you will love them.

Serves: 2

Ingredients:

- 4 ripe peaches, pitted and cut in half
- 2 tablespoons honey
- 2 scoops raspberry sorbet
- 2 scoops vanilla ice cream

Directions:

1

Heat a grill pan over medium heat.

2

Place the peaches on the grill and cook 6-8 minutes until tender and browned.

3

Place the peaches into serving bowls and top with raspberry sorbet and ice cream.

4

Drizzle with honey and serve right away.

Quick and Easy Recipes That Even Kids Can Make

If you have a curious child like most parents do, you know that the kitchen is a place where children like to explore; therefore, they spend a lot of time watching their mums or dads chop ingredients, cook, boil, roast, or bake; they love tasting and even enjoy getting involved in the cooking process.

Here are a few quick and easy recipes that even kids can make—they are that easy! They have common ingredients that are easy to find at any time of the year, and they require only basic cooking techniques, which makes them very safe. However, I don't advise you to leave your child alone in the kitchen, cooking. You should always be there to watch him!

Just don't take away this joy, which is all about the food and the cooking process. It's a matter of finding the right recipes and using the right techniques to make cooking as safe and enjoyable as possible for your child.

Pita Pockets

These pita pockets are really fun and can be stuffed with basically anything. Your taste is all that matters!

Serves: 4

Ingredients:

- 4 mini pita breads
- 4 tablespoons cream cheese
- ¼ cup grated cheddar
- ¼ cup chopped parsley
- 1 ripe tomato, sliced

Directions:

1

Carefully make a small pocket in each pita.

2

Stuff them with cream cheese, cheddar, parsley, and tomato and serve right away.

Egg Cups

This is a great way to cook eggs that even kids can make. As long as you supervise the oven, they can have fun preparing the eggs, adding their favorite seasonings, and then serving the eggs with bread or potato fries if they want to.

Serves: 2

Ingredients:

- 2 eggs
- 1 tablespoon chopped chives
- Salt, pepper to taste
- 2 tablespoons butter
- 1 red bell pepper, cored and diced

Directions:

1

Place the butter in two ramekins.

2

Crack open the eggs and drop them into the ramekins as well.

3

Top with chives and bell pepper, then season with salt and pepper.

4

Bake the eggs in the preheated oven at 400°F for 10 minutes or less, depending how soft you want the eggs to be.

5

Serve right away.

Colorful Quinoa

Quinoa is an interesting seed that has a high nutritional profile, and kids should be consuming it because it has fiber and many other nutrients that are beneficial for children. If you make it colorful and fun and let them help cook it, they will surely at least try it.

Serves: 2-4

Ingredients:
- 2 cups cooked quinoa
- 1 red bell pepper, cored and diced
- 1 yellow bell pepper, cored and diced
- 2 tomatoes, cubed
- 1 cup green peas
- Salt, pepper to taste
- ¼ lemon, juiced
- 2 tablespoons olive oil
- ¼ cup chopped parsley

Directions:

1

Combine the quinoa with the vegetables.

2

Add salt and pepper to taste, then stir in the lemon juice, olive oil, and parsley; mix gently.

3

Serve the salad right away.

Nutella Popsicles

Nutella is a treat for children; they absolutely adore it. But you don't have to let them eat it all the time in its purest form because it can also be diluted and used to make desserts that are less sugary and much more healthy. These popsicles are one of the best options, especially during summer.

Serves: 6

Ingredients:

- 1 cup Nutella
- 1 cup full cream milk
- 1 cup heavy cream
- ½ teaspoon vanilla extract

Directions:

1
Combine all the ingredients in a blender.

2
Pulse until smooth and well blended.

3
Pour the mixture into your popsicle molds and freeze for a few hours before serving.

Gazpacho – Cold Tomato Soup

This soup only requires some blending, and if your child is old enough, he can surely do it. It is a fresh and nutritious soup that will revitalize your children during the summer, for sure.

Serves: 2-4

Ingredients:

- 1 pound tomatoes
- 1 cucumber
- 1 celery stalk
- 1 garlic clove
- 4 tablespoons olive oil
- 1 white bread slice, soaked in water, then drained
- ½ cup ice cubes
- 2 green onions, chopped
- 2 oz. mozzarella, cubed
- Salt, pepper to taste

Directions:

1
Combine the tomatoes, cucumber, celery, garlic, olive oil, bread, and ice cubes in a blender.

2
Pulse until well blended and smooth.

3
Season with salt and pepper and pour into serving bowls.

4
Top with green onions and mozzarella cubes just before serving.

Date and Coconut Bites

Dates have a high fiber content and are delicious, sweet, and healthy. Combined with coconut, they yield delicious little bites that are perfect for when your kids need an energy boost.

Serves: 2-4

Ingredients:

- 2 cups pitted dates
- 2 cups desiccated coconut
- ½ teaspoon vanilla extract
- 2 tablespoons cocoa powder
- 1 cup desiccated coconut for rolling

Directions:

1

Combine the dates with the coconut, vanilla, and cocoa powder in a food processor.

2

Pulse until well blended.

3

Wet your hands and form the mixture into small balls, then roll each of them through the coconut.

4

Serve right away or store in an airtight container for up to 4 days.

Carrots and Herbed Cream Cheese Dip

Carrots have high beta-carotene content, and we all know how great they are for our eyes and skin. Kids tend to love them because they are crunchy and sweet, but you can step out of your comfort zone and try carrots with a delicious cream cheese dip as well.

Serves: 2-4

Ingredients:

- 1 pound young carrots
- 1 cup cream cheese, softened
- 2 tablespoons buttermilk
- 2 tablespoons chopped parsley
- 1 tablespoon chopped dill
- 2 basil leaves, chopped
- Salt, pepper to taste
- 2 tablespoons olive oil

Directions:

1

Mix the cream cheese with the buttermilk, parsley, dill, basil, and olive oil.

2

Add salt and pepper to taste and mix well.

3

Serve the carrots by dipping them into the cream cheese dip.

Warm Peanut Butter and Banana Sandwich

Your children will love this for sure, and you can let them make it all by themselves. It's an easy and quick recipe for a quick snack in the afternoon. And, if I may add, it is also fairly healthy.

Serves: 2

Ingredients:

- 4 slices whole wheat bread
- 2 tablespoons peanut butter
- 1 ripe banana, sliced
- 2 tablespoons cocoa nibs

Directions:

1

Spread the peanut butter on two slices of bread.

2

Top with banana slices and cocoa nibs, then cover with the other two slices of bread to form sandwiches.

3

Heat a grill pan over medium heat and place the sandwiches on the grill for 2-3 minutes on both sides.

4

Serve right away.

Cheesy Black Bean Tacos

A bit spicy, but loaded with nutrients, these tacos are a real delight with all that cheese melting over the delicious beans.

Serves: 4

Ingredients:

- 8 taco shells
- 1 can black beans, drained
- ½ cup mild salsa
- ½ cup canned diced tomatoes
- 1 cup grated cheddar cheese

Directions:

1

Combine the beans with the salsa and tomatoes in a saucepan and bring to a boil.

2

Cook for 5-8 minutes on medium heat.

3

To serve, spoon the hot beans into taco shells. Top with grated cheese and serve right away.

Pizza Sandwiches

These sandwiches are a great substitute for pizza. They are just as flavorful and gooey as real pizza, but much easier to make.

Serves: 2

Ingredients:

- 4 slices white sandwich bread
- ¼ cup tomato sauce
- 4 cherry tomatoes, halved
- 2 thick slices cheese of your choice
- 2 basil leaves, shredded

Directions:

1. Spread the tomato sauce on all 4 slices of bread.
2. Top two of the slices with tomatoes, cheese, and basil, then cover with the other 2 slices of bread to form the sandwiches.
3. Place them in a sandwich maker and press until the cheese is melted.
4. Serve the sandwiches right away.

Peanut Butter Dip with Apple and Pears

This dip is amazing with slices of apples and pears. They are all ingredients that have an earthy or nutty aroma, and therefore, work together perfectly, creating a snack that tastes like dessert but is healthy.

Serves: 2-4

Ingredients:

- ¼ cup peanut butter
- 2 tablespoons marshmallow cream
- ¼ cup Greek style yogurt
- 2 apples, sliced
- 2 pears, sliced

Directions:

1

Combine the peanut butter with the marshmallow cream and yogurt in a bowl.

2

Mix well.

3

Serve by dipping the apple and pear slices into the peanut butter cream.

Hot Chocolate Mix

Grown-ups love hot chocolate, and kids love it even more. However, the store-bought mix is not very healthy. The best option is to make it at home, where you know exactly what ingredients are included and you are able to control the final taste.

Serves: 6-8

Ingredients:

- 1 cup powdered sugar
- 1 cup coco powder
- ½ cup dry milk powder
- ¼ teaspoon cinnamon powder
- 1 pinch salt

Directions:

1
Combine all the ingredients in a glass jar and mix them well.

2
To prepare the chocolate, place a few tablespoons into a glass and pour in hot water or milk.

3
Store the mix in a glass jar with a lid for up to 1 month.

Dark Chocolate Clusters

Crunchy and loaded with chocolate, these clusters are addictive. If you're using dark chocolate, they are also quite healthy, especially since the chocolate is a good source of antioxidants.

Serves: 2-4

Ingredients:

- 1 cup corn flakes
- 10 oz. dark chocolate, melted

Directions:

1

Combine the two ingredients in a bowl.

2

Drop spoonfuls of the mixture on a baking sheet and refrigerate a few minutes until set.

3

Serve right away.

Homemade Cereals

Breakfast is crucial for kids. That is where they get their energy for the day, and it should be as healthy and nutritious as possible. Cereals are a great option for breakfast, and if you let your kids help you make them, they will have fun and love it even more.

Serves: 6-8

Ingredients:

- 4 cups rolled oats
- 1 cup chopped almonds
- ½ cup raisins
- ½ cup dried cranberries
- ½ cup dried apricots, chopped
- ½ teaspoon cinnamon powder
- ½ cup dark chocolate chips

Directions:

1

Combine all the ingredients in a bowl and mix until evenly distributed.

2

Transfer into a sealed glass jar and store for up to 2 months in a dark, cold place.

3

To serve, pour in to a bowl and top with milk, yogurt and honey, or maple syrup.

Marshmallow Pops

Marshmallows always make me think of childhood. Those chewy little bites make children happy, but they can also be used to make various desserts that are fun and delicious. These pops are so easy to make that you can let your kids customize them all they want.

Serves: 4-6

Ingredients:

- 1 bag large marshmallows
- ½ cup colorful sprinkles
- 10 oz. dark chocolate, melted
- ½ cup chopped walnuts

Directions:

1

Place each marshmallow on a wooden skewer.

2

Dip the marshmallows into chocolate first, then sprinkle with walnuts or sprinkles and place on a parchment paper.

3

Refrigerate a few minutes to set, then serve.

Chocolate Chip Parfait

Kids sure love chocolate. That is a fact, but you can combine it with healthier ingredients to make sure your children are eating a balanced diet. It's a very nice trick if you want to make them eat more nutritious foods than sweets.

Serves: 2-4

Ingredients:

- 2 cups Greek style yogurt
- 2 tablespoons honey
- ½ cup dark chocolate chips
- 1 cup rolled oats
- 1 cup chopped walnuts

Directions:

1

Combine the yogurt with the chocolate chips and honey in a bowl.

2

Layer the oats, yogurt, chocolate chips, and walnuts in individual serving bowls or glasses.

3

Serve the parfait right away or refrigerate a few hours until serving.

Chocolate Chip and Raspberry Snacks

These little snacks are so delicious and fragrant. It's such a good idea for parties, and they are so easy to make. Children will surely have fun putting these together.

Serves: 4-6

Ingredients:

- 1 pound fresh raspberries
- 10 oz. dark and white chocolate chips

Directions:

1

Take each raspberry and stuff it with a chocolate chip.

2

Repeat until all raspberries are stuffed; serve fresh.

3

It's such a fun and great idea, isn't it?

Italian Flavored Popcorn

This recipe is so versatile! You can use basically any flavoring, from Cajun to curry, or herbs and spices—the sky is the limit!

Serves: 2-4

Ingredients:

- 4 cups popcorn
- ¼ cup grated Parmesan cheese
- ½ teaspoon dried oregano
- ½ teaspoon dried basil
- 1 pinch salt
- ½ teaspoon salt

Directions:

1

Combine all the ingredients in a large bowl.

2

Toss around to evenly coat the popcorn and serve right away.

Beet and Berry Smoothie

What I love about this smoothie is the fact that it hides the healthy beets under the fragrant and intense aroma of the berries. Now you know for sure that your kids will eat their veggies for the day! Also, don't forget that brightly colored fruits and veggies are rich in antioxidants.

Serves: 2-4

Ingredients:

- 1 raw beet, juiced
- 1 cup mixed berries
- 1 cup plain yogurt
- 2 cups almond milk
- 2 tablespoons honey

Directions:

1

Combine all the ingredients in a blender.

2

Process until well blended and smooth, then pour the smoothie in glasses and serve right away.

Strawberry and Spinach Smoothie

I know that kids and spinach aren't usually mentioned in the same sentence, but teaching them about healthy foods and healthy eating has to begin at an early age and continue gradually. Explain to your child what spinach is and show him recipes that taste great despite having spinach. Let them see for themselves how delicious spinach can be!

Serves: 2-4

Ingredients:

- ½ cup spinach
- 1 cup fresh strawberries
- 1 ripe banana
- ½ cup plain yogurt
- 2 cups almond milk
- 2 tablespoons chia seeds
- ¼ cup ice cubes

Directions:

1
Combine all the ingredients in a blender and process until well blended and smooth.

2
Pour the smoothie in glasses and serve right away.

Easy and Quick Recipes for Parties

It can be a real struggle to plan a party, and food is the main worry, especially if you're on a budget and have little time at your disposal to organize everything. In these conditions, you have two options: to have it catered or do it yourself. Catering is expensive, so there you are, left with having to do everything yourself, either from scratch or using little shortcuts to help you. This chapter offers you just that—quick and easy recipes that will save your life when organizing a party. They take less than 15 minutes to make from start to finish, but they all taste great and are fun to eat.

Your guests will appreciate the tortilla wheels or the banana popsicles, as well as the red wine punch or the fragrant watermelon and basil bites. It may sound overwhelming, but you can do this! Delight your guests with amazing food and an amazing party!

Tortilla Wheels

These tortilla wheels can be done one or two days ahead and kept in the fridge, then sliced just before the party. You can use any vegetables you want for the filling, and they will taste amazing and look fun.

Serves: 4-6

Ingredients:

- 4 flour tortillas
- ½ cup cream cheese, softened
- 4 canned roasted bell peppers, sliced
- 1 bunch parsley, coarsely chopped
- Salt, pepper to taste

Directions:

1

Spread the cream cheese over the tortillas.

2

Top with roasted bell peppers and parsley, then sprinkle with salt and pepper.

3

Roll the tortillas tightly and wrap them in plastic wrap.

4

Refrigerate a few hours up to two days, then slice into 1-inch thick slices.

5

Arrange them on a platter and serve.

Quick Banana Popsicles

You won't find an easier popsicle recipe than this one. And despite being so easy to make, they taste amazing. They are creamy and rich, refreshing and nutritious, and perfect for parties—especially kids' parties.

Serves: 4

Ingredients:

- 2 ripe bananas, halved and frozen
- 1 cup dark chocolate chips, melted
- ½ cup chopped walnuts
- 4 wooden skewers

Directions:

1

Place the banana halves on wooden skewers.

2

Dip each banana piece in chocolate, then quickly roll it through walnuts.

3

Serve the popsicles right away.

Marshmallow Sauce and Fruit Skewers

Fruit skewers are delicious and fun on their own, but this sauce really makes them shine with how fluffy and airy it is.

Serves: 4

Ingredients:

- 1 ripe banana, sliced
- 2 kiwi fruits, peeled and sliced
- 1 cup fresh strawberries
- 1 cup cantaloupe cubes
- 1 cup cream cheese, softened
- ½ cup marshmallow fluff
- ½ teaspoon vanilla extract
- 1 teaspoon lemon zest

Directions:

1. Place the fruits on wooden skewers, layering them to look as beautiful as possible.
2. To make the sauce, combine the cream cheese with the marshmallow fluff, vanilla, and lemon zest.
3. Spoon the sauce into a serving bowl and place it on a large platter.
4. Arrange the fruit skewers around the bowl of sauce and serve.

Mini Pita Pizzas

Pizza is a classic food for parties, but slicing a big pizza and serving it is not that easy at a party with so many people around. These mini pizzas will save the day. They taste just like a traditional pizza, but take little time to make and come in a small and fun size.

Serves: 6

Ingredients:

- 6 mini pita breads
- 4 tablespoons pesto sauce
- 1 cup shredded mozzarella
- 2 ripe tomatoes, sliced

Directions:

1

Spread the pesto on all pita breads.

2

Top with shredded cheese and tomato slices.

3

Place them on a baking tray and bake at 400°F for 8-10 minutes.

4

Serve them fresh, warm or cool.

Sticky Rice Balls

Asian flavors are interesting and definitely worth introducing to your party menu. These balls are not only easy to make but also easy to serve and look so fun with all the different coatings.

Serves: 6

Ingredients:

Rice balls:
- 2 cups cooked rice
- Salt, pepper to taste
- 1 teaspoon rice vinegar
- ½ cup black sesame seeds
- ½ cup white sesame seeds
- ¼ cup chopped chives

Sauce:
- ¼ cup light soy sauce
- 1 teaspoon rice vinegar
- 1 teaspoon honey
- 2 green onions, chopped
- 2 tablespoons chopped cilantro

Directions:

1. Combine the rice with the vinegar, then season with salt and pepper.
2. Form small balls of rice and roll all of them through the black sesame, white sesame, and chopped chives.
3. Place them on a platter.
4. To make the sauce, combine all the ingredients in a bowl.
5. Serve the rice balls with the sauce for dipping.

Red Wine Punch

A party without drinks is not a party, wouldn't you agree? And this punch tastes great without being too alcoholic or overwhelming. It's a balanced, fruity drink, perfect for both informal and elegant parties.

Serves: 10

Ingredients:

- 1 bottle red wine
- 1 cup brandy
- ½ cup orange liqueur
- 1 cup fresh orange juice
- 1 cup cranberry juice
- 2 oranges, sliced
- Ice cubes for serving

Directions:

1. Combine all the ingredients in a large punch bowl.
2. Mix well and serve with ice cubes.

Mexican Vegetarian Sushi

This recipe is a fusion of sushi and Mexican flavors. These sushi bites will surely kick off the party with their spiciness.

Serves: 4-6

Ingredients:

- 6 flour tortillas
- 1 ½ cups cream cheese, softened
- 1 cup hot salsa
- 1 avocado, peeled and cut into sticks
- 1 red bell pepper, cored and sliced
- 1 yellow bell pepper, cored and sliced
- Salt, pepper to taste

Directions:

1

Spread the cream cheese over each tortilla.

2

Evenly spread the salsa, then place the avocado slices and bell peppers in the center of each tortilla.

3

Roll the tortillas tightly, then slice them in 1 ½inch-thick slices.

4

Serve right away.

Deviled Eggs

Deviled eggs are a classic and make a great party appetizer. They are easy to make and so versatile. You can literally add any seasoning you like to the filling and have a whole new recipe every time.

Serves: 6

Ingredients:

- 6 hard-boiled eggs, sliced lengthwise
- ½ cup mayonnaise
- 2 tablespoons lemon juice
- 2 tablespoons sour cream
- 2 tablespoons chopped chives
- Salt, pepper to taste

Directions:

1. Remove the egg yolks and place them in a bowl.
2. Mash them with a fork, then stir in the mayonnaise, lemon juice, sour cream, and chives.
3. Season with salt and pepper and mix well.
4. Spoon the filling back into each egg half and place them all on a platter.
5. Serve fresh.

Spicy Cheese Fondue

Cheese fondue is a real delicacy, trust my word! That melting, gooey cheese is great to serve with either slices of apple or pear or sticks of toasted bread. No matter what options you choose, cheese fondue will be a hit at your party.

Serves: 2-4

Ingredients:

- 1 cup heavy cream
- 2 tablespoons butter
- ½ teaspoon chili flakes
- 1 cup grated Monterey Jack cheese
- 1 cup grated cheddar cheese
- 1 pinch nutmeg
- Fruits or bread to serve

Directions:

1

Combine the heavy cream with the butter and chili flakes in a saucepan and bring to the boiling point.

2

Remove from heat and add the cheeses and nutmeg.

3

Mix well until the cheese is melted.

4

Transfer the mixture into a special bowl for fondue that is placed over hot water or even a lit candle to keep it warm and melted.

5

Serve with slices of fruits or toasted bread.

Two-Layer Hummus

Hummus is a common dip, but layering it is not! What you get with this unique recipe is a flavorful and colorful dish, delicious and filling, that tastes great with tortilla chips or toasted bread.

Serves: 4-6

Ingredients:

Basil hummus –
- 1 can chickpeas, drained
- 2 tablespoons tahini paste
- ¼ lemon, juiced
- ¼ cup olive oil
- ¼ cup basil leaves
- 2 tablespoons chopped cilantro
- 2 tablespoons pine nuts
- Salt, pepper to taste

Roasted bell pepper hummus –
- 1 can chickpeas, drained
- 2 tablespoons tahini paste
- 4 roasted bell peppers, drained
- 2 tablespoons lemon juice
- 2 tablespoons olive oil
- Salt, pepper to taste

Directions:

1. To make the basil hummus layer, combine all the ingredients in a blender.
2. Pulse until well blended and smooth, then season with salt and pepper to taste.
3. Spoon the hummus into a large glass serving bowl.
4. To make the bell pepper hummus, mix all the ingredients in a blender and process until well blended and smooth.
5. Add salt and pepper to taste, then spoon the hummus over the first layer of basil hummus.
6. Serve right away.

Kalamata Olive Bruschetta

This Italian dish called bruschetta may be simple, but it tastes great. The flavors are fresh and intense, and it only takes a few minutes to make. Easy and delicious!

Serves: 12

Ingredients:

- 12 slices Italian bread, toasted
- 1 cup pitted Kalamata olives
- ¼ cup pitted black olives
- 6 sun-dried tomatoes
- 2 tablespoons olive oil
- 10 basil leaves, shredded

Directions:

1

Place the sun-dried tomatoes in a blender and pulse until smooth.

2

Add the olives and olive oil and pulse just until ground, but not turned into a paste yet.

3

Spread the mixture on each slice of bread and top with shredded basil.

4

Place the bruschetta on a platter and serve right away.

Olive Oil and Fresh Ricotta Bruschetta

This recipe is so simple! It relies on the intense and incredible aroma of a good extra virgin olive oil and the freshness of ricotta cheese. That is all!

Serves: 6

Ingredients:

- 6 slices Italian bread, toasted
- 1 cup fresh ricotta
- 4 basil leaves, chopped
- Salt, pepper to taste
- ¼ cup extra virgin olive oil

Directions:

1. Combine the ricotta with the basil, then season with salt and pepper.
2. Spread the ricotta mixture on each slice of bread.
3. Place the bruschetta slices on a platter and drizzle each slice with plenty of olive oil.
4. Serve right away.

Spicy White Bean Dip with Tortilla Chips

This dip is perfect for an informal party amongst friends. It's easy to make and has common ingredients, but it tastes so good with all those spices and a touch of garlic!

Serves: 4-6

Ingredients:

- 2 cups canned white beans, drained
- 2 garlic cloves, chopped
- ¼ cup olive oil
- ½ teaspoon Sriracha sauce
- 1 pinch nutmeg
- 1 pinch allspice powder
- ¼ teaspoon smoked paprika
- 2 tablespoons lemon juice
- 1 bag tortilla chips

Directions:

1

Combine the beans with the garlic, olive oil, Sriracha, allspice, paprika, and lemon juice in a blender.

2

Process until well blended and smooth, then spoon the dip into a serving bowl.

3

Serve the dip with tortilla chips.

Basil, Watermelon and Feta Bites

You would be surprised to learn how good watermelon, basil, and feta taste together. I think a party is a great occasion to try new, unusual recipe combinations, and this is one of them!

Serves: 4-6

Ingredients:
- 1 small seedless watermelon, cubed
- oz. feta cheese, cubed
- ½ cup basil leaves
- ¼ cup olive oil
- 2 tablespoons lemon juice

Directions:

1

Combine the basil with the olive oil and lemon juice in a bowl and pulse until well blended.

2

Place the watermelon and feta on a platter.

3

Drizzle them both with the basil sauce and serve fresh.

Parmesan and Basil Tomato Bites

Being creative in the kitchen is a must! And this recipe is one of the most creative you can find. Just take some cherry tomatoes and fill them with a delicious Parmesan stuffing. Easy, fresh, and delicious!

Serves: 4

Ingredients:

- 1 pound cherry tomatoes
- 1 cup grated Parmesan cheese
- 1 cup cream cheese
- 1 pinch chili flakes
- ¼ cup chopped basil

Directions:

1

Take each tomato and scoop out part of the flesh, leaving the skin intact if possible.

2

Stuff the tomatoes with the cheese mixture and place them on a platter.

3

Serve fresh.

Endive Boats

Endives are amazing vegetables in salads, and they can successfully be used for these delicious and flavorful boats, filled with cream cheese, herbs, and roasted peanuts. This is a recipe that combines more tastes and textures in one and offers an interesting eating experience.

Serves: 10

Ingredients:

- 3 endives, split leaf by leaf
- 2 cups cream cheese
- ¼ cup chopped cilantro
- ¼ cup chopped basil
- 2 ripe tomatoes, diced
- ½ cup roasted peanuts, chopped
- Salt, pepper to taste

Directions:

1. Combine the cream cheese with the cilantro and basil, salt and pepper to taste, and mix well.
2. Place the endive leaves on a platter.
3. Drop spoonfuls of cream cheese in each endive leaf.
4. Top with diced tomatoes and chopped peanuts.
5. Serve them right away.

Scallion Goat Cheese Balls

Goat cheese is creamy, rich, earthy, and absolutely delicious in this combination, trust me! Just keep reading the recipe, then try it and see for yourself. These balls are addictive.

Serves: 4-6

Ingredients:

- 10 oz. goat cheese, softened
- ½ cup crushed pineapple
- 2 scallions, chopped
- 1 cup ground walnuts
- Salt, pepper to taste

Directions:

1. Mix the goat cheese with the pineapple and scallions.
2. Add salt if needed and a pinch of freshly ground pepper.
3. Form small balls and roll them all through the ground walnuts.
4. Place them on a platter and serve right away.

Potato Chip Snacks

Using shortcuts is allowed when you're throwing a party, although, these snacks taste so good that you will want to make them as often as possible.

Serves: 10

Ingredients:

- 1 large bag potato chips
- 1 pound tomatoes, diced
- 1 avocado, peeled and diced
- ½ cup chopped cilantro
- 2 garlic cloves, chopped
- ½ shallot, chopped
- Salt, pepper to taste
- 1 pinch cayenne pepper

Directions:

1

Combine the tomatoes with the avocado, garlic, and shallot.

2

Add the cayenne pepper as well as salt and black pepper to taste and mix well.

3

Spoon the mixture on the potato chips and place them all on a serving platter.

4

Serve fresh.

Spicy Pecans

What would a party be without spicy snacks? These are great to kick off the fun, and I bet people will keep asking for them. They can get addictive; they are that good!

Serves: 6-8

Ingredients:

- 1 pound pecans
- 1 teaspoon smoked paprika
- 1 teaspoon sweet paprika
- ¼ teaspoon cayenne pepper
- 1 teaspoon garlic powder
- 4 tablespoons coconut oil

Directions:

1

Melt the coconut oil in a skillet.

2

Stir in all the spices, then add the pecans.

3

Sauté them for 10 minutes, stirring often.

4

Transfer them on a platter and serve chilled.

Blue Cheese and Pear Crostini

Crostini are similar to bruschetta. They have the same taste, but a crunchier texture. This version is simple, but fresh and delicious, great for those who love blue cheese.

Serves: 6

Ingredients:

- 6 slices Italian bread, toasted
- 6 small slices blue cheese of your choice
- 1 ripe pear, cored and finely sliced
- 2 tablespoons lemon juice

Directions:

1

Sprinkle the pear slices with lemon juice to avoid oxidation, then place the slices on each slice of bread.

2

Top with blue cheese and arrange on a platter.

3

Serve as fresh as possible.

Walnut and Cheese-Stuffed Figs

These stuffed figs are delicious raw, but once you roast them slightly, the cheese begins to melt and infuses them with a delicious salty taste. The walnuts add richness, so the final taste is classy.

Serves: 12

Ingredients:

- 12 large dried figs
- 12 small pieces of walnuts
- 12 dollops goat cheese

Directions:

1

Carefully cut and open the dried figs.

2

Stuff them with cheese and walnuts and place them on a baking tray.

3

Bake at 400°F for 10 minutes.

4

Serve right away.

Conclusion

Diet change is not an easy process, but it can be done if you have the will and the means to do it, despite not having much time for cooking. Don't let the issue of time take over your life and keep you from what you should value the most in life: health, family, and friends. You can make time for everything, healthy eating included, and the food you make can actually taste great, even if it took just 15 minutes. These are all facts, and you will never know until you try!

So put that apron on and get cooking because there is nothing stopping you from being a vegetarian and having a busy life at the same time. Meat is not the center of your diet, so don't let it define you! Fresh fruits and vegetables are the way to go if you want a healthy body and a healthy, creative mind!